T0023822

PROFILING A CRIMINAL

Using Science to Seek Out Suspects

CHERITON
CHILDREN'S BOOKS

Published in 2023 by **Cheriton Children's Books**
1 Bank Drive West, Shrewsbury, Shropshire, SY3 9DJ, UK

© 2023 Cheriton Children's Books

First Edition

Author: Sarah Eason
Designer: Paul Myerscough
Editor: Louisa Simmons
Proofreader: Ella Hammond

Printed in China

Please visit our website,
www.cheritonchildrensbooks.com
to see more of our high-quality books.

CONTENTS

CHAPTER 1

PROFILING A CRIMINAL

Tracking and catching criminals is never as simple as it seems in television shows and movies! It involves hours of painstaking work and a lot of time and effort. Science is one of the greatest tools that modern crime fighters use, but although the police have various scientific methods of collecting and **analyzing evidence**, they may not be enough to crack a case. This is why the science of crime profiling is so important.

A Brand New Science

Crime profiling is one of the newest methods in crime science. Crime profilers study where, when, and why crimes are **committed**. By doing this, crime profilers can learn a lot about who may have carried out a crime, and why it was committed.

Some crime profilers are experts in the way criminals think, while others specialize in spotting patterns in where crimes take place. Some advise the police about how to reduce crime, while others are brought in to help catch dangerous criminals.

Many would-be profilers attend college to learn the skills they need to help the police catch dangerous criminals.

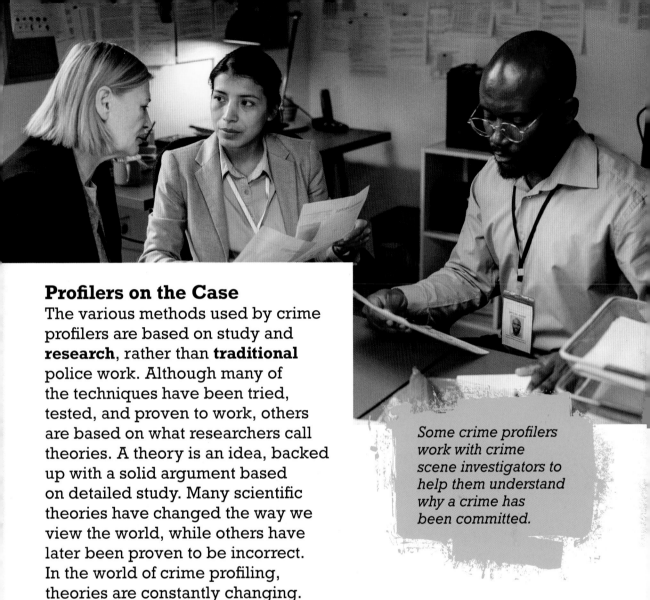

Profilers on the Case

The various methods used by crime profilers are based on study and **research**, rather than **traditional** police work. Although many of the techniques have been tried, tested, and proven to work, others are based on what researchers call theories. A theory is an idea, backed up with a solid argument based on detailed study. Many scientific theories have changed the way we view the world, while others have later been proven to be incorrect. In the world of crime profiling, theories are constantly changing.

Some crime profilers work with crime scene investigators to help them understand why a crime has been committed.

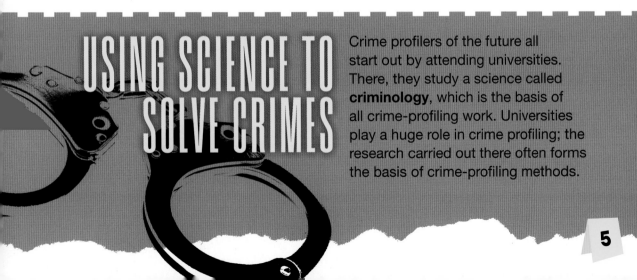

USING SCIENCE TO SOLVE CRIMES

Crime profilers of the future all start out by attending universities. There, they study a science called **criminology**, which is the basis of all crime-profiling work. Universities play a huge role in crime profiling; the research carried out there often forms the basis of crime-profiling methods.

The Science of Crime

The basis of all crime profiling is criminology. This is the scientific study of crime. Many of the crime profiling techniques used by the police are based on criminology. Criminology is not a new science. The term was first used by an Italian lawyer and university professor named Raffaele Garofalo, in 1885. Since then, the science of criminology has developed into a vast subject, with many different theories. People who study criminology are known as criminologists. It is their job to look at where and how frequently crimes take place, and why criminals break the law.

Some criminologists spend time talking to prisoners to try and find out why they turned to crime.

CRIME SCIENCE

One of the oldest ideas in criminology is Rational Choice Theory. This is the idea that criminals make a conscious choice to commit crimes. Supporters of this theory say that the way to **deter** people from choosing to commit crimes is to offer tougher punishments.

The Causes of Crime

Some criminologists look in detail at the things that **influence** criminal behavior, such as the world around us, where people live, and how much money they have. Others specialize in specific forms of crime. Criminologists study every aspect of crime in order to try and explain why crime happens, and more importantly, how criminal acts can be stopped.

Different Ideas

Because criminology is such a broad science, criminologists often disagree on the causes of crime. Over the years, many different theories have been put forward to explain criminal behavior. This is a natural part of science. New evidence may prove old theories to be incorrect, while scientists often disagree about what the evidence tells us. Ultimately, theories are just ideas—it is how they are used in the fight against crime that is important.

Ideas About Crime

Over the years, criminologists have put forward many different ideas to explain the causes of crime. Some are **controversial**, others have been changed and **adapted** over time. The cause of crime is one of the longest-running areas of discussion. The very first criminologists, known as the "Classical School of Criminology," believed that people choose to commit crime.

Turning to Crime

Later, criminologists of the "Positivist School" argued that people turn to crime due to forces beyond their control, such as losing their job, knowing other criminals, or living in run-down areas. In the early twentieth century, criminologists expanded on this idea. They believed that being poor and not doing well at school were the reasons why most people turned to crime.

Some criminologists believe that having more police officers on the streets deters criminal behavior.

What Is a Criminal Mind?

Since the early twentieth century, many theories have been put forward to explain why people turn to crime. Some criminologists believe that certain people have a "criminal mind," and are more likely to do terrible things. Other criminologists believe that children **inherit** "criminal traits" from their parents.

A Changing World

Over time, attitudes toward certain crimes have changed, so people may not believe, or care, that they are breaking the law when committing these crimes. For example, some criminologists argue that crime has increased because people are willing to break the law to get the latest must-have clothes and gadgets.

Many criminologists think that poverty is linked to crime, because people are more likely to be driven to commit crimes due to need.

CRIME SCIENCE

Criminologists have developed an idea called "Strain Theory." They argue that when money is tight, jobs are hard to come by, and people feel pressured by the strain of day-to-day life, they are more likely to turn to crime as a way out of their problems.

The Effects of Crime

One of the latest ideas in criminology theory is victimology. This is the study of **victims** of crime, how the crime affects them, and whether their actions put them at risk of attack. Some of the ideas put forward by victimologists are highly controversial. One theory is that some people are more likely to become victims of crime because of certain things they are likely to do. This could be doing a specific type of high-risk job, walking alone late at night, or being particularly friendly to strangers. This is an unpopular idea because it suggests that victims of crime make themselves a target for criminals, and therefore in some way may attract criminal acts.

CRIME SCIENCE

Some victimologists are employed by the government to study what effect crime has on victims, and how the **legal system** can make victims' lives more bearable. Others study crime data to try to figure out what sort of people are more likely to be the victims of crime.

Victimologists often talk to victims of crime, to find out how they have been affected.

Today, many people are far more vocal about how they feel about crime and its effects.

Understanding Crime

Victimology includes studying how people are affected by the crimes committed against them. That information can then be used by people in the police force, courts of law, and governments to better understand how victims feel about crime, and what type of punishments should be given to people who carry out crimes.

Victims' Rights

Today, more consideration is given to the rights of victims of crime. In the United States, victims are encouraged to go to court to explain how a crime has affected them. The victims are allowed to speak about what has happened to them before the judge decides on a suitable punishment for the criminal.

BUILD A BETTER WORLD

Many criminologists believe that the way people behave is influenced by their surroundings. They think that there is a direct link between where people live and whether they commit crimes.

The Poor Become Criminals?

There is a close link between crime levels—how many crimes happen—and poverty. More crimes happen in poor areas of cities. While some criminologists think that this is because there are fewer people with jobs and money is tight in these areas, **environmental** criminologists believe that the condition of buildings, the number of boarded-up properties, and how many parks and open spaces are present there is just as important.

Nature Fighting Crime

Some environmental criminologists think that the number of trees in an area has an effect on the crime rate. Research in Portland, Oregon, has proven that levels of crime are significantly lower in areas where there are more large trees.

A Crime-Free Plan

Studies by environmental criminologists have also suggested that the height of backyard fences, the size and shape of windows, and the type of street lighting used can also have an effect on crime rates. Because of this, town planners and **architects** have begun working with environmental criminologists when designing buildings and housing estates. They hope that by doing this, they will deter criminals from targeting the areas and people who live there.

Preventing Crime Through Design

The idea of trying to reduce crime through the design of buildings and neighborhoods is called Crime Prevention Through Environmental Design (CPTED). Ideas regularly used by CPTED specialists include widening sidewalks to encourage more people to walk and bicycle around, adding trees to public areas, installing **surveillance** cameras, and making street lighting much brighter.

Crime Science

In a recent crime study research program, researchers analyzed data from 301 cities in the United States with populations greater than 100,000 to see what effect a greener environment has on crime rates. Researchers discovered a clear link between more green space in cities and a significantly reduced risk of crime against property and violent crimes against people.

A neighborhood with plenty of trees and green spaces is less likely to be targeted by criminals than a built-up inner-city neighborhood.

CHAPTER 2

A REVOLUTIONARY SCIENCE

Although criminology theories are the basis of all crime profiling, they do not always have a practical use for tackling crime. The same cannot be said of crime analysis, an area of criminal science that has **revolutionized** police work.

Where and When

Crime analysis is examining all the available information about crimes in order to identify and predict trends. Police forces must record information about every crime reported, including where it was, who the victim was, and what sort of crime took place.

This data is stored on vast banks of computers and it is of great use to crime analysts. Not only can they use it to figure out crime rates, but they can also pinpoint exactly where crimes are taking place.

Police forces often operate a higher level of patrol at night, when they know that crime is more likely to occur.

A greater police presence is often seen in areas where high-tech crime analysis shows significant numbers of crimes.

Informed Police

Police forces all over the world use crime analysts to help them police the streets more effectively. If they know where, when, and what sort of crimes take place, then they can try to reduce crime. For example, if they know that there are more street crimes at night in a particular area, they can send out more police patrols at night to deter criminals. If the **statistics** show that drug users commit a lot of crimes, then police forces can put more **resources** into trying to catch drug dealers.

A Head for Figures

Crime analysts are often people who are very good at math. Every day, they have to trawl through **software** programs full of numbers and statistics to try and find trends. A trend is a pattern—for example, it could be a rise in violent crime or a reduction in the number of teenagers committing crimes.

Joining the Dots

Crime analysis is now being used by police forces to identify the biggest crime problems in their area, so they can tackle them head-on. This approach is called "problem-oriented policing." It is a method in which police forces combine crime analysis reports with the thoughts of police officers on the ground.

Smart Policing

In problem-oriented policing, police officers are encouraged to use systems such as CompStat to identify crime trends—for example, by observing a rise in **vandals** breaking windows or convenience-store robberies, they may more easily find the cause of the crimes. By dealing with the root of the problem, the number of crimes of that type should drop.

People Power

Most police forces that use problem-oriented policing try to involve the public. They actively encourage people to tell them about the problems in their area, often by holding weekly community meetings. In most areas where problem-oriented policing has been used, crime rates have dropped and confidence in the police has risen. When relations between the police and the public are at their best, crime is most likely to drop.

Problem-oriented policing has been successfully used to reduce crime rates in a number of US cities.

TRUE CRIME STORY

Police in San Diego used the problem-oriented policing approach to reduce drug dealing in part of the city. After talking to residents and an apartment block's manager, they were able to identify drug dealers and users, and either arrest them or **evict** them from their homes.

TRACK CRIME

Crime analysis is a complicated process, but one that is changing the way the police tackle crimes. Using specially designed computer software, crime analysts can track the location, type, and **frequency** of crimes committed.

Pioneering Police

The New York Police Department (NYPD) pioneered the use of crime analysis. In 1994, the NYPD started using CompStat. CompStat used computer software to **compile** reports of all the crimes committed in New York City. NYPD software allowed crime analysts to view maps of the city, which showed the location of the crimes. The system also included data on the police response, such as how many officers were sent to a crime scene. As part of the process, representatives from each of the city's 76 area precincts met to go through the crime-analysis information.

Crime Cutting

CompStat is a huge success. According to NYPD officials, it has helped cut crime in the city dramatically. It also played an important role in cutting the number of murders from more than 1,100 in 1995 to 414 in 2012. Because of the system's success, it has since been adopted by police forces all over the United States, Canada, and the United Kingdom (UK). By knowing all of the facts about where, when, and how often crimes happen, the police can more accurately manage their response to reported crimes.

Crime Science

Police forces in the United States, Canada, and the UK now allow the public to see the location and details of crimes collected using the CompStat process. Using the website www.crimereports.com, people can get updates of where, when, and what type of crimes are being reported.

CompStat has helped police forces around the world find, arrest, and lock up many criminals.

CHAPTER 3

WHERE AND WHY

Geographic profiling is the "where" of modern policing. It uses advanced software to look at where crime is happening, either to identify patterns of criminal behavior or to help solve serious cases, such as serial killings or chains of robberies.

Old Idea, New Science

Geographic profiling is concerned with two things —where and why crimes take place. It is based on the old idea of crime mapping. In crime mapping, detectives would stick pins into a large map to see if there were any patterns between crime scenes and where evidence had been found.

Geographic profiling has helped police track down criminals, such as robbers and muggers who commit crimes in a small area.

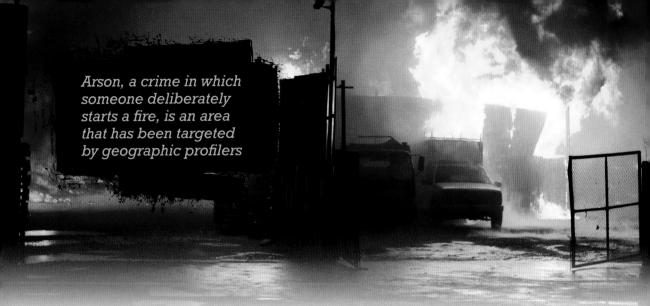

Arson, a crime in which someone deliberately starts a fire, is an area that has been targeted by geographic profilers

Crime Connections

Geographic profilers suggest that most criminals will commit their crimes in an area that they know well. This could be near where they live, an area in which they work, or somewhere they regularly go in their free time. Geographic profiling is most often used to help police with different crimes that may be connected.

Geographic profilers are specialists in spotting what they call "patterns of **offender** behavior." For example, if a serial killer was at large and all of the victims had been found close to bars, it would suggest that the killer had picked them at random when out at night. In cases of serial crimes, such as murders or arson, more often than not there are patterns in the way that criminals behave. These patterns are not always obvious, so geographic profiling can help find the criminal.

TRUE CRIME STORY

Geographic profiling was first used in 1981, during the hunt for a serial killer nicknamed the "Yorkshire Ripper." A **forensics** and mapping expert named Stuart Kind told the police he believed the killer lived in one of two places. When the Ripper, Peter Sutcliffe, was arrested two weeks later, Kind was proven right.

Mapping Crimes

The backbone of geographic profiling is crime mapping. Although now quite advanced thanks to the use of computers, it has been used by police forces for many years for a number of reasons. In the early days of crime mapping, police stuck pins into large maps. Originally, crime mapping was used in serious cases with multiple crimes, to help narrow down the search for evidence. By looking at the location of the pins in the map, police could identify the best areas to look for clues.

New and Improved

In recent years, crime mapping has become more sophisticated. Today's crime analysts use a type of computer software called Geographic Information Systems (GIS) to keep track of the location of crimes, spot trends, and advise police about crime hotspots.

Part of CompStat

The GIS used by crime analysts allows them to look at many different types of information. They can, for example, compare the location of crimes with the locations of schools, betting establishments, bars, nightclubs, and housing areas. By doing so, analysts can begin to understand the underlying causes of crime, and in turn suggest solutions to the problems. Crime mapping is a vital part of the CompStat system used by many police forces, and it has also been used in problem-oriented policing.

When a crime is committed, every detail about it must be carefully recorded and logged in the CompStat system for use in preventing further crimes.

CRIME SCIENCE

Crime analysts who use crime mapping spend a lot of their time comparing many different types of information. In order to guide the police, they compile presentations showing the exact **location** of specific crimes over a set period of time, the locations of certain types of crimes, and how the police responded.

STORE AND SEARCH

The days of sticking pins in maps mounted on the walls of police stations are long gone. Today, crime mapping and geographic profiling is carried out using advanced computer software programs. Modern crime-mapping software is based on GIS. These advanced computer programs combine mapping software with databases. A database is a program that allows users to store and search through enormous amounts of data both quickly and easily.

Software to Solve Serial Murders

Using GIS software, crime analysts can search for information, which will then be displayed on a map, or series of maps. There are now a number of specialist geographic-profiling software systems available to crime analysts.

Crime Science

One of the most cutting-edge geographic-profiling programs is GeoCrime. The system allows users to see the social and demographic profile of every residential area in incredible detail. For example, users can see if a large number of students live in an area, or if families are the main occupants. It can show how rich or poor people living there are, how connected the streets are, and can also show how busy an area is at different times.

*Dr Kim Rossmo's geographic-profiling computer program was designed to help solve **serial** murder cases.*

Systems Solving Crimes

The first specialist geographic-profiling computer program was developed by Canada's Dr Kim Rossmo. It formed the basis of later systems, one of which is Rigel Analyst. According to its makers, this program has a high success rate and can narrow down the likely home of a wanted criminal. It is said to be 95 percent accurate. This means that it is correct in 95 out of 100 crimes. Another popular program used by many police forces is CrimeStat. This has features similar to Rigel Analyst, but can also help analysts figure out how far criminals travel to carry out their crimes.

Serial Killer Hunter

When hunting for serial killers, many police forces use a geographic-profiling program called Gemini. Gemini has been designed specifically to figure out which crimes may belong to a series, or are the work of the same criminal. It even ranks crimes in order of how likely they are to be part of a series.

Profiling Problems

Although popular, geographic profiling is not always as successful as other methods. According to critics of the theory, this is because it has serious limitations. The biggest problem with geographic profiling is that it is concerned only with the locations of crimes. While some criminals may carry out their crimes in a certain area, or in a pattern, this is not always the case. If detectives base their investigations on geographic-profile findings that turn out to be wrong, they will have wasted a lot of time and money. What is more, in that time, the criminals carry out even more crimes.

Long-Distance Crime

Often, geographic-profiling systems also overlook the fact that some criminals are prepared to travel large distances to carry out their crimes, which makes profiling unhelpful. Another worry that critics have is about the computer software itself. The results of geographic profiling will only ever be as good as the software used, and the information entered into the database. If the information is out of date, incorrect, or even misleading, the geographic profile will be inaccurate.

Serious Crime Tool

Critics say that although geographic profiling can be a useful tool in serious crime cases, it should only ever be used with other methods, such as evidence gathering and interviewing **witnesses**. However, despite its limitations, geographic profiling does get results.

Geographic profilers do not take into account the fact that some criminals commit crimes in several areas. If a serial killer murdered their victims in several areas or states, geographic profiling would be of little use.

TRUE CRIME STORY

Raymond Lopez was arrested for robbing more than 200 houses in California after police used geographic-profiling software to predict where Lopez lived. More police patrolled the area, leading to the robber's arrest.

POLICE LINE DO NOT CROSS   POLICE LINE DO N

LINE DO NOT CROSS   POLICE LINE DO NOT C

INSIDE A CRIMINAL'S MIND

The best-known area of crime profiling is offender profiling. Also known as **psychological** profiling, offender profiling has been featured in many movies and television series. Offender profiling is the process of trying to figure out who committed a crime and why they did it, based on an understanding of criminal behavior. Offender profilers try to identify criminals by analyzing the crime, how it was committed, and any other relevant case evidence.

Police investigators use the information in a criminal profile to help them with their investigations.

Criminal profiles can help police better understand offenders and the crimes they commit.

Studying the Clues

Criminals may leave clues at the crime scene about the type of person they are, and how they think. Offender profilers also look in close detail at the choices criminals make before and after a crime, such as how well it was planned and the methods used to carry out the crime. The choices made can also offer clues about the people who made them.

Finding Criminals

Offender profilers often begin their careers as psychologists, scientists who specialize in understanding human behavior. They do not work on all cases and, in general, the police use them only to help catch very serious criminals. To help police, they must create a detailed description of the type of person who may have committed the crime.

A Varied Job

Offender profilers divide their time between studying case evidence in order to create psychological profiles, teaching police detectives about basic profiling techniques, and learning more about how and why crimes are committed. They spend most of their time in an office, and rarely visit crime scenes.

Psychological profilers work closely with detectives while investigating murder cases.

Developing the Science

The psychological profiling of criminals is not a new development. It has been used in different forms since the nineteenth century. Over the years, a number of famous profilers have helped develop the science behind the technique.

Jack the Ripper

The first offender profiler was a doctor named Thomas Bond. During the 1880s, he studied the crimes of a famous murderer nicknamed "Jack the Ripper." After looking in detail at the Ripper's crimes, he figured out that the killer was likely to be a quiet, middle-aged man who was "strong, composed, and daring."

Adolf Hitler

During World War II, which lasted from 1939 to 1945, the US government asked psychologist Dr Walter C. Langer to create an offender profile of the Nazi leader, Adolf Hitler. To create his profile, Langer studied Hitler's books and listened to recordings of his speeches. Langer predicted that Hitler would kill himself if he lost the war. That is exactly what happened in April 1945.

Finding a Bomber

In the 1950s, a psychologist named James A. Brussel helped police track down a **terrorist** who had planted bombs in New York City over a 16-year period. Brussel studied the case files and figured out that the bomber was likely to be a "heavy," middle-aged mechanic who once worked for the Consolidated Edison power company. The description helped the police catch George Metesky, whose appearance and background accurately matched Brussel's profile.

TRUE CRIME STORY

Offender profiling helped investigators track down one of the United States' most dangerous serial killers, Ted Bundy. Offender profiling specialist Dr Richard B. Jarvis provided police with a description that accurately predicted Bundy's age, characteristics, and above-average intelligence.

Ted Bundy is one of the most high-profile killers of all time.

Five-Phase Process

In the United States, offender profiling is carried out using a special five-phase technique called the Federal Bureau of Investigation (FBI) profiling method. This was developed by two of the fathers of modern offender profiling—John E. Douglas and Robert Ressler.

Examine the Evidence

The FBI profiling method uses five different stages to create an accurate profile of a dangerous criminal, usually a murderer. First, profilers examine all the available case information and evidence, from crime-scene photos and victim profiles to police reports and witness statements. This is known as the **"assimilation** stage."

Classify the Criminal

The second stage is called the "classification stage," in which profilers decide if the criminal is organized or disorganized. Organized criminals often plan their crimes in detail, while disorganized criminals do not plan and leave a lot of evidence.

Sometimes, criminals leave signature clues at a crime scene, which can help profilers understand them.

It is important that any evidence, no matter how small, found at a crime scene is collected and documented so it can be used in the assimilation stage.

Before and After

In the third stage, profilers focus on the criminal's behavior before and after the crime. The idea is to try and figure out the exact **sequence** of events, in order to learn not only how the crime was committed, but also what it says about the criminal's personality.

When that stage is complete, the profilers look for the criminal's "signature." This is anything the criminal does at the scene of the crime that is different or unusual, and may give a clue about the way they think. The final stage of the FBI method is to create a profile for detectives to use.

CRIME SCIENCE

John E. Douglas is one of the most successful FBI criminal psychologists of all time. During the 1970s, he worked at the FBI's Behavioral Sciences Unit (BSU), where he taught his famous FBI method of profiling. He retired in 1995, but is still asked by police forces to help in the hunt for serial killers.

*Profilers from the BAU are regularly asked by detectives investigating serious cases to go to crime scenes, and to help them compile questions for interviews with **suspects**.*

Special Department

The FBI has a special department dedicated to psychological analysis and offender profiling. It is part of the National Center for the Analysis of Violent Crime (NCAVC), and it is called the Behavior Analysis Unit (BAU). The Unit is based in Virginia and takes responsibility for most offender profiling undertaken by the FBI.

The Best Profilers

Most of the Unit's staff members are experienced criminal profilers who specialize in violent crimes such as murder, crimes against children, or terrorism. The Unit's scientific approach to crime and great knowledge of criminal behavior has helped bring many dangerous criminals to justice over the last 20 years.

Called in to Help

When police forces and FBI departments are hunting killers or other dangerous criminals, they often contact the BAU for help. Sometimes, the BAU sends profilers around the country to help investigators. Other times, they offer advice over the telephone. They also offer training for FBI agents in the basic principles of offender profiling.

Cracking Tough Cases

The BAU specializes in "criminal investigative analysis." Criminal investigative analysis involves looking closely at serious crime, criminal behavior, and also the investigation itself, to help detectives crack difficult cases. The Unit carries out its tasks using a number of different methods, from offender profiling and crime analysis to advising detectives on how best to manage **manhunts** for serial killers.

Questions for Criminals

One of the ways in which BAU profilers use their knowledge of criminal behavior is to advise detectives on what to ask suspected criminals during police interviews. They often devise a series of questions that are most likely to result in a confession from the criminal.

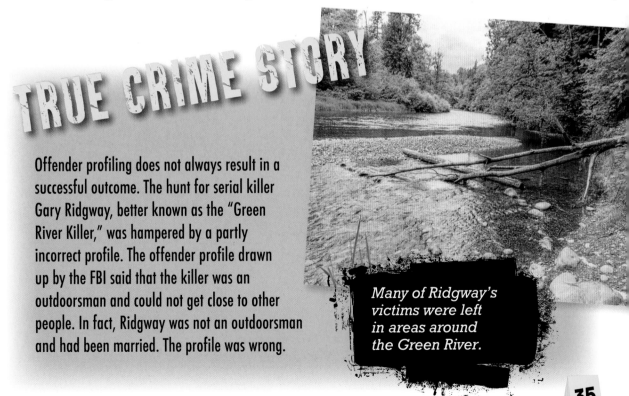

TRUE CRIME STORY

Offender profiling does not always result in a successful outcome. The hunt for serial killer Gary Ridgway, better known as the "Green River Killer," was hampered by a partly incorrect profile. The offender profile drawn up by the FBI said that the killer was an outdoorsman and could not get close to other people. In fact, Ridgway was not an outdoorsman and had been married. The profile was wrong.

Many of Ridgway's victims were left in areas around the Green River.

FIND THE LINK

One of the tasks often performed by BAU crime profilers is linkage analysis. This technique brings together elements of criminal and geographic profiling to figure out if a series of crimes is linked.

Connecting Crime and Criminal

Linkage analysis is a method used by profilers and police detectives to figure out whether a series of crimes was committed by the same criminal. For example, police could be investigating a series of killings in different states that were carried out over a long period of time. They may not look like they are connected, but by carrying out detailed linkage analysis, criminal profilers may be able to prove that they were the work of the same criminal. When carrying out linkage analysis, criminal profilers will try to use their understanding of criminal behavior to spot patterns that link the crimes together.

Where and When

Today, linkage analysts will often carry out geographic profiling as part of the process. This is to see whether there are additional links or clues in the location of the crimes, or where bodies were discovered in murder cases.

Last Resort

Generally, linkage analysis is a last resort for detectives working on murder cases. It is used only in rare cases where evidence is limited. Often, crimes are solved using DNA evidence, which can provide clues about a criminal's **identity**, or fingerprint marks left at the crime scene. When this type of evidence does not exist, detectives may turn to linkage analysis.

Crime Science

Police in Canada developed a software system to carry out linkage analysis. Called the Violent Crime Linkage Analysis System (ViCLAS), it has so far helped prove links between serial criminals in a multitude of crimes ranging from **homicides** to kidnapping. The system is now being used around the world.

The tiniest piece of evidence could provide a link between the crime being investigated and the criminal.

Problems with Profiling

Although offender profiling is hugely popular with the public and is often used by the police, critics say it is not very **reliable**. They say it is not nearly scientific enough, and when profiles prove to be incorrect, it can waste valuable police time.

Making Mistakes

The biggest problems with offender profiling happen when profilers make mistakes. If they assess all the evidence and tell police to look for a particular type of person, more often than not, detectives will put great faith in their opinion. If the profile turns out to be incorrect, the police will be searching for the wrong person and may even arrest someone who is totally blameless.

Not Enough Science

Critics of offender profiling say that it is impossible to draw conclusions about somebody's personality, background, and appearance from what they do when committing a crime. They argue that detectives should not read too much into the way someone behaves before and after they commit a crime, because they may be acting differently due to the pressure of the situation.

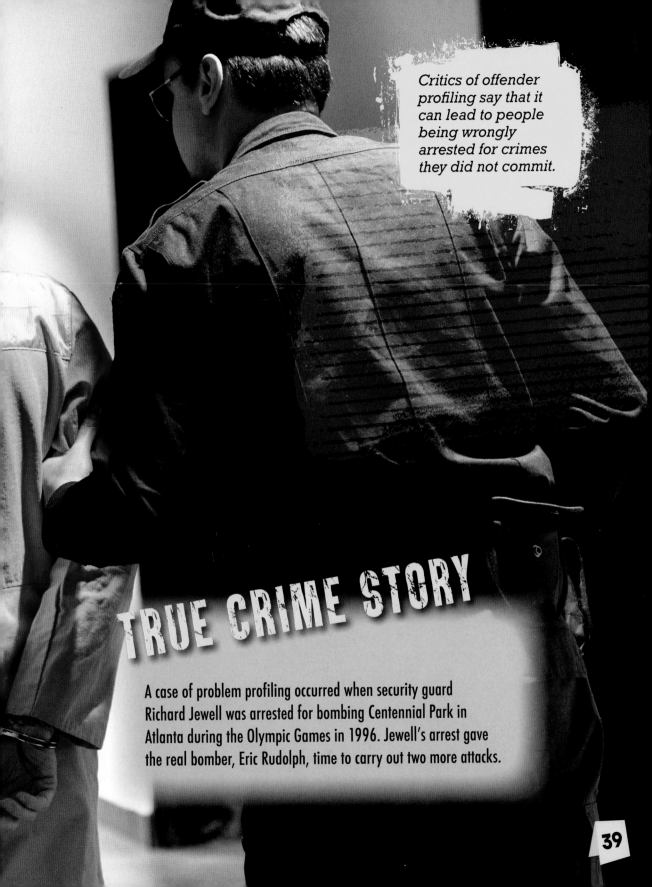

Critics of offender profiling say that it can lead to people being wrongly arrested for crimes they did not commit.

TRUE CRIME STORY

A case of problem profiling occurred when security guard Richard Jewell was arrested for bombing Centennial Park in Atlanta during the Olympic Games in 1996. Jewell's arrest gave the real bomber, Eric Rudolph, time to carry out two more attacks.

As a new science, crime profiling is by no means perfect. However, every year new ideas are put forward and cutting-edge techniques are developed. All of the methods, techniques, ideas, and theories of offender profiling have good and bad points. Criminologists and crime profilers understand this, and are working hard to increase their understanding of criminals, their behavior, and the science of catching them.

Comparing Criminals

One of the latest developments in criminology is the idea of comparative criminology. This is the study of crime across different countries and groups of people, for example, those who earn a certain amount of money, or follow a certain religion. The idea is to try and identify differences and similarities between crime rates and types of crime. By doing so, criminologists may be able to figure out the major causes of crime, and how they could be tackled in the future.

Crime is complicated—it arises because of many different conditions. Today, people better understand the causes of crime, and many leading criminologists believe the best way to address it would be to improve the lives of those living in deprived areas.

By comparing crime trends and statistics from different parts of the world, criminologists hope that they can learn more about the causes of crime.

Stopping Crime

One idea that has gained popularity in recent years is crime prevention as a way of lowering crime rates. The idea is to stop, or prevent, people from turning to crime in the first place. Many criminologists have spent years studying which approaches work, including fighting poverty. The world's leading criminologists have worked together to list the best ways to prevent crime. They suggest that countries should join forces in tackling the global drug trade and focus more on the problems that cause crime, such as poverty.

CRIME SCIENCE

Some of the busiest crime profilers are forensic psychiatrists. These are scientists with a deep knowledge of how the human mind works.

They are often used in court cases to pass judgment on whether or not criminals have any mental illnesses that may influence their behavior.

THE FUTURE OF PROFILING

In the last 30 years, crime profiling has gone from an experimental technique to one of the cornerstones of modern policing. It has revolutionized the way crimes are investigated.

Cutting Crime

Crime mapping helps police forces reduce crime and better plan their response to urgent calls from the public. Geographic profiling has helped detectives pinpoint the whereabouts of many violent criminals, murderers, and **arsonists**. Thanks to psychological offender profiling, detectives now better understand the way criminals behave, and how they may think. Crime analysis allows police to quickly spot crime trends, while problem-oriented policing has improved many lives by cutting crime.

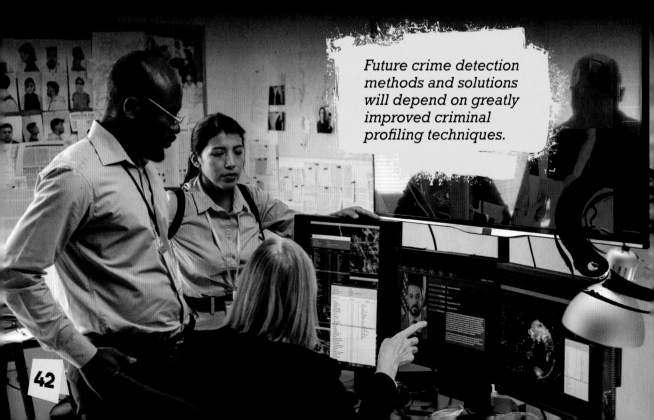

Future crime detection methods and solutions will depend on greatly improved criminal profiling techniques.

Shaping the Future

Many policing advances would not have happened without modern profiling techniques. Recent crime rates in many major cities, such as New York City and Los Angeles, have been falling, thanks in part to new profiling techniques.

Perfecting Profiling

Crime profiling is not without fault. We need to remember that it is a new science. All of its methods are constantly being looked at, altered, and improved. Ongoing research by criminologists and psychologists will help shape the future of all detective work. Mistakes may still be made, but far more criminals will be caught.

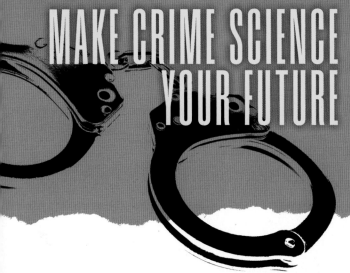

MAKE CRIME SCIENCE YOUR FUTURE

Criminal profiling is a fascinating area to work in. It involves an in-depth understanding of the human mind and how it works, and a love of investigative research. If you think you have what it takes to work in this cutting-edge science field, overleaf you'll find a career guide that could one day help you profile a criminal.

COULD YOU PROFILE A CRIMINAL?

Crime dramas win record viewings, and these gripping shows have inspired many to enter the world of crime science and investigation. It is an amazingly exciting field to work in, with new, game-changing developments emerging all the time.

The work of criminal profilers can be instrumental in helping solve crimes, and the work itself is varied, fascinating, and constantly evolving, or changing. The chart below shows some of the areas of work and responsibilities of this exciting role.

Criminal Profiler

- Identify behavior patterns
- Understand investigative strategy, crime analysis, and interviewing techniques
- Perform personality assessments and geographic profiling
- Study human behavior and characteristics
- Conduct research, analyze data, and form conclusions
- Advise police officers and investigators
- Read and write reports
- Provide evidence in court

To pursue a career in criminal profiling, follow this simple flowchart.

Choose relevant subjects at school

Focus on the school subjects needed to earn a bachelor's degree, which will be required if you want to work in criminal profiling. Sciences and math are often required for a psychology degree, and biology and chemistry will be required for a forensics degree.

After school, earn a bachelor's degree

A criminal profiler will need a bachelor's degree for many entry-level jobs. You should major in criminology, criminal justice, psychology, or **sociology** for your bachelor's degree. A combined degree in psychology and criminal justice would be very helpful.

Complete a law enforcement training program

Before working in law enforcement, profilers need to complete training at a law enforcement academy. There may be requirements to enter this role, such as a clean criminal record, so check that you meet the conditions first. Working as a police officer in an investigative role will give you the skills and experience you will need to begin a career as a criminal profiler.

Earn a master's degree or doctorate

Some roles will also require a master's degree or doctorate in criminal justice, forensic psychology, behavioral sciences, or a related field. A psychology-related degree is ideal. Some criminal profilers choose to earn a master's degree or doctorate once in the role.

Apply for jobs

Most criminal profilers are employed by the FBI in the BAU and work in the NCAVC in Quantico, Virginia. Profilers will need seven to 15 years of work experience before applying to work for the FBI. Recruitment is not limited to the FBI. There are also job opportunities to be found with local law enforcement.

GLOSSARY

adapted changed to better suit something

analyzing studying something carefully in order to better understand it

architects people who design buildings

arsonists people who deliberately start fires

assimilation the process of taking in and fully understanding information

classification to group things in order to make sense of them

committed carried out a crime

compile to gather or put together

controversial describes something that causes heated discussion and disagreement

criminology the study of crime and criminals

deter to discourage someone from doing something

environmental related to the environment, or the natural world

evict to force a person to move from their home

evidence information, objects, or substances that are related to a crime

forensics applying scientific knowledge to solve criminal and legal problems

frequency how often something happens

homicides murders

identity who someone is

influence to have an effect on, or change

inherit to be given something by one's parents

legal system the system of laws and lawmaking

location the place something is found or where something occurs

manhunts searches for a criminal

offender a person who has committed a crime

psychological related to the mind

reliable can be trusted or depended upon

research studies and investigations to find out more about something

resources money, people, and time needed to carry out work

revolutionized changed beyond recognition

sequence the order in which things happen

serial describes crimes that are similar and take place one after the other

sociology the study of human behavior

software computer programs that tell a computer what to do

statistics numerical information that provides important data

surveillance keeping a close watch over someone or something

suspects people suspected of carrying out crimes

terrorist a person who carries out acts of terror

traditional describes something that has been done for a long time, or was done in the past

vandals people who damage or destroy things such as buildings

victims people who have been injured, harmed, or killed by other people

witnesses people who saw something, such as a crime, take place

FIND OUT MORE

Books
Cooper, Chris. *Forensic Science: Discover the Fascinating Methods Scientists Use to Solve Crimes* (DK Eyewitness). DK Children, 2020.

Ross, Melissa. *Forensics for Kids: The Science and History of Crime Solving, With 21 Activities* (For Kids). Chicago Press Review, 2020.

Toner, Jaqueline and Claire Freeland. *Psychology for Kids: The Science of the Mind and Behavior.* Magination Press, 2021.

Websites
Learn more about crime science at:
www.explainthatstuff.com/forensicscience.html

Find out what happens at a crime scene investigation and how specialists such as crime profilers assist investigations at:
www.howstuffworks.com/csi.htm

Find out more about criminology at:
https://kids.britannica.com/students/article/ criminology/273857

Publisher's note to educators and parents:
All the websites featured above have been carefully reviewed to ensure that they are suitable for students. However, many websites change often, and we cannot guarantee that a site's future contents will continue to meet our high standards of educational value. Please be advised that students should be closely monitored whenever they access the Internet.

INDEX

About the Author

Sarah Eason is an experienced children's book author who has written many science books for children. She loves watching crime-detective shows, and after researching and writing this book is more fascinated than ever by the world of criminal profiling and forensic science.